JANET CARIJA BRANDT

Folk Art Animals

25 Fanciful Appliqué Designs

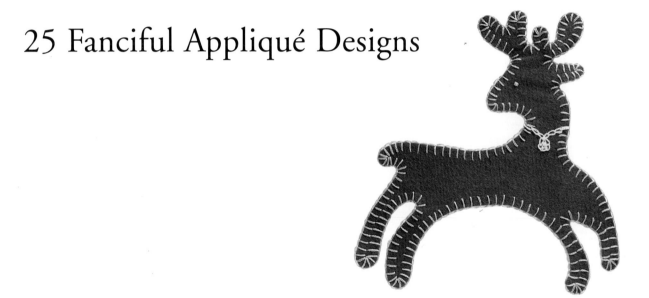

Martingale
& COMPANY

BOTHELL, WASHINGTON

ACKNOWLEDGMENTS

Being able to recognize and publicly thank the many people who have helped me with this book is one of the most satisfying parts of this process.

For the gorgeous samples in the gallery, I would like to thank Millie Churbuck and Lucy Brown; the "Little Quilts" ladies, Alice Berg, Mary Ellen Von Holt, and Sylvia Johnson; Debby Eads; Deb Haggard; Brian Haggard; Betsy Harris; and Holly Sieck. Special thanks to Jan Paul for the many hours of cutting out little fusible animals.

A big thank-you to Pat Smith and Terry Volk at Kings Road for beautiful wool flannel to work with. And thanks to Janet Bounce at National Nonwovens for introducing me to the wonderful wool felts.

To Martingale and Company, a thank-you to Melissa Lowe, Janet White, and the entire talented staff.

And most of all, a big thank-you to Chris, without whom the many hours of uninterrupted sewing, designing, and writing would not be possible.

CREDITS

Technical Editors . . . . Janet White, Melissa A. Lowe
Design and Production Manager . . . . Cheryl Stevenson
Cover and Text Designer . . . . Trina Stahl
Copy Editor . . . . Liz McGehee
Illustrator . . . . Laurel Strand
Illustration Assistant . . . . Robin Strobel
Photographer . . . . Brent Kane

MISSION STATEMENT

We are dedicated to providing quality products and service by working together to inspire creativity and to enrich the lives we touch.

Folk Art Animals: 25 Fanciful Appliqué Designs
© 1998 by Janet Carija Brandt
Martingale & Company, PO Box 118
Bothell, WA 98041-0118 USA

Printed in Canada
03 02 01 00 99 98   6 5 4 3 2 1

The information in this book is presented in good faith, but no warranty is given nor results guaranteed. Since Martingale & Company has no control over choice of materials or procedures, the company assumes no responsibility for the use of this information.

Library of Congress Cataloging-in-Publication Data
Brandt, Janet Carija,
Folk art animals : 25 fanciful appliqué designs / Janet Carija Brandt
p.   cm.
ISBN 1-56477-222-5
1. Appliqué—Patterns.   2. Patchwork—Patterns.   3. Quilts.
I. Title
TT779.B74   1998
746.46'041—dc21   98-4509
                                                                    CIP

Contents

Introduction

FOLK ART ANIMALS is all about choices: lots and lots of fun choices. Choose one animal or any combination of animals. Choose one fabric or any combination of fabrics. Choose one color or any combination of colors. The choices go on and on. *Folk Art Animals* is also about how to make those choices so you can complete a beautiful project that suits your style, your talents, your budget, and your time—in other words, *your* needs.

My fabric choices for the projects in this book include traditional woven 100%-cotton, 100%-wool flannel, and wool-blend felt. If your fabric stash includes only cotton and that is what you most enjoy working with, by all means use cotton. If you have new or recycled pieces of wool flannel, this might be the perfect opportunity to use it. Wool-blend felt is a great new option that is very easy to work with.

The design choices in *Folk Art Animals* are so numerous, you will feel like a kid in a candy store. First, you have twenty-five animal designs to choose from. The animals range from domestic to exotic, from chickens to peacocks. Use the animals in individual blocks or together in a larger composition. Use them separately, in multiples, or in any combination. Next, choose from the pages of options, where you'll find images and accessories to round out the story in your quilt. The most versatile option is that of the penny rug. Several of the proj-

ects in the book are contemporary penny rug interpretations. You will learn about traditional penny rugs with their plain, round, coinlike shapes and simple tongue borders, as well as the wild and creative variations in penny shapes and decorative borders.

There are lots of techniques to choose from, too. Try my mini-fuse technique for easy cotton appliqué, or a basic pin-and-sew technique for the wool flannel and felt. Try fabric markers, decorative rotary cutters, and embroidery stitches to embellish your projects. Whether you do your work by hand or with a machine makes no difference in quality. A needle and thread is a tool just as a sewing machine is a tool. The care you put into your work is what distinguishes a great piece from a lesser piece.

A gallery packed with colorful inspiration follows step-by-step instructions for eight projects. Full-size templates are included for each of the animals, the options, the pennies, and the borders. Read and enjoy, then begin making your choices.

Choosing a Fabric

COTTON

Cotton is the fabric most familiar to quilters. So many wonderful choices are available at your local quilt shop or are just a phone call away through many mail-order sources. I recommend woven 100%-cotton fabrics. The colors, prints, textures, and inspirations are endless. Cotton is a plant fiber and is easy to cut, piece, and appliqué in crisp, accurate designs.

For all of the cotton quilts in this book, I used an easy, fun technique that I call mini-fuse. It has the ease of fusible appliqué without the stiffness and difficulty associated with hand stitching through fusible web. Most of my stitching is hand-work, so I am very concerned about the kinds of repetitive movements I make with my hands. The mini-fuse technique is very user-friendly. It seals the cotton edges and holds the appliqué pieces in place long enough for you to add the blanket stitch. Find the complete instructions on pages 11–13. All measurements for cotton are based on prewashed 44"- to 45"-wide fabric. A fat quarter is fabric pre-cut to 18" x 22".

WOOL

Wool has a long tradition of use in quilts and rugs. It is delightful to work with. Wool offers textures and tactile qualities that you won't find in any other fabric. Use woven 100%-wool flannel for the best results. Just think of a favorite wool skirt. That is the weight and feel of fabric you are looking for. Wool now appears in many quilt shops as well as stores that carry dressmaker fabrics.

Working with wool is simple. Begin by pre-washing all wool, whether new or recycled. Machine wash in warm water with regular laundry detergent on a normal cycle. Machine dry. The wool will shrink slightly and come out of the dryer fluffy. This shrinking is a felting technique called fulling.

FELT

Another option for your projects is a wool-blend felt. I like to use a wool/rayon blend made up of 20% to 50% wool fibers, which is becoming more readily available. Felt is not a woven fabric. It is made of wool fibers packed together in a dense mat.

Wool felt is very different from the 100%-acrylic felt and is worth seeking out. The edges stay crisp whether cut with a straight edge or a decorative cut-ter. Decoratively cut edges do not have to be fin-ished with a blanket stitch, greatly reducing the amount of handwork necessary. Wool-blend felts can also be hand dyed for unlimited color choices.

Wool felt takes on a totally different feel when it is machine washed and dried. The surface becomes textured and the hand is very soft. If you iron washed felt, you will lose the pebbly texture and it will return to its usual smooth finish. Many commercially dyed wool-blend felts are not color-fast and need to be dry-cleaned.

Choosing a Design

ANIMAL DESIGNS

Most of the twenty-five animals in this book fit in a 5" square block. Several of the larger animals fit in 5" x 7½" blocks, and the largest block is 5" x 10" to accommodate the tall giraffe. Keep in mind that the block sizes are only a suggestion, and you may use the animal designs in any size setting you like. The animals are not always in correct proportion to each other. You may enlarge or reduce the animals to suit your taste, but remember, a big part of the charm of folk art is its complete unawareness of the formal laws of proportion and scale.

PENNY-RUG DESIGN

To understand the origin of the penny rug, we have to start with the early nineteenth-century meaning of the word *rugg*. A rugg was a coarse covering for a bed, a chest, or a table. Ruggs were never intended for floors. Textiles were too precious, too labor-intensive to produce, to simply put down on a floor and wear out. Textiles were proudly displayed and highly prized for their warmth and beauty.

All of that gradually changed as ready-made fabrics became more available. Bits and pieces of fabrics and scraps from old clothing were put back to work as table and bed coverings and put on the floor as well. During the second half of the nineteenth century, penny rugs made their first appearance. Coin rugs, dollar rugs, and mosaic rugs are other names for this type of rug. Penny rugs got their name from the coin that was most often used as a pattern for cutting the many circles needed for one rug. Circles of many sizes were needed, and coins or any available round objects of the right size were used for the patterns. The fabric circles were stacked two or three high, each circle in the stack a little smaller than the circle below. These penny stacks were secured in the center with a French knot or cross-stitch to hold the layers together until they were stitched in place on the background fabric. The size and shape of the rug would depend on where it was to be used, how much fabric was available, and how the stacks were arranged.

Some penny rugs were finished with a petal or tongue border. Tongue borders were popular, as were entire rugs made of petal or tonguelike shapes, their rounded edges finished with the blanket stitch and their straight edges secured to the background fabric. Penny rugs did not have a batting and were not quilted, but they usually had a backing fabric. For more ideas, see page 33.

DESIGN APPLICATIONS

Now you know about the animals and you know about penny rugs. So, what about the design?

Your design can be just one animal.

Your design can be just one animal repeated many times.

Your design can include all the animals, as in "The Lord God Made Them All" (see photo on page 32), or you can make two of each and march them into an ark.

Your animals can stay in the little blocks they were designed in.

Your animal blocks can lie scattered about like photos in an album.

Your animals can inhabit an environment of your own making.

Your design can be a penny rug.

Your design can combine animals, pennies, and words.

Your design can be all words and have a simple bound border.

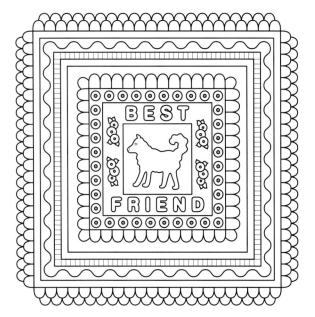

Your design can be a sampler of borders.

Your design can be a pillow, table runner, window valance, dust ruffle, book jacket, or banner for your favorite typing teacher.

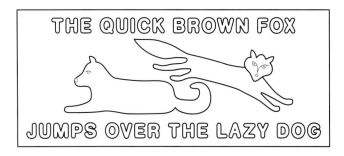

Your design may incorporate any of the following options, such as variations of animal eyes:

Animal wings and attire:

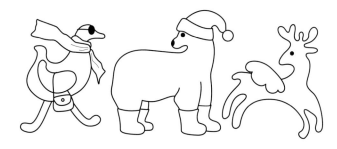

Pennies:

Single   Double   Triple   Or more!

Flower   Star   Heart   Cotton yo-yo

Blanket stitch   Chain stitch   Combination of stitches

Buttons   Nine patch   Crazy quilt   Pinked center

Pumpkin   Horseshoe   Shamrock   Flower

Borders:

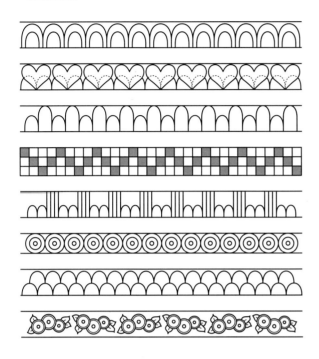

Details such as flags, animals in carts, a fence, and clouds:

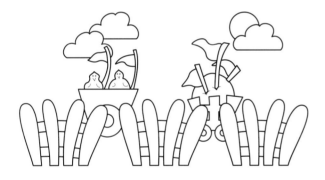

Trees:

Or your design may include quotes and proverbs, such as:

Enough is as good as a feast.

—ENGLISH PROVERB

Man may work from sun to sun, but woman's work is never done. —ANONYMOUS

Hickety pickety, my black hen,
She lays eggs for gentlemen.

—ANONYMOUS

Hands are the heart's landscape.

—POPE JOHN PAUL II

A door is what a dog is perpetually on the wrong side of. —OGDEN NASH

Love one another. —JOHN 13:34

A merry heart doeth good like a medicine.

—PROVERBS 17:22

Life was meant to be lived.

—ELEANOR ROOSEVELT

Be cheerful while you are alive.

—PTAHHOTPE, 2400 B. C.

Choosing a Technique

EMBROIDERY STITCHES

All of my appliqué work and added embroidered details are done with two strands of embroidery floss and a #8 crewel needle. These are the supplies that give me the look I want my work to have. Silk ribbon, crewel yarn, perle cotton, or any other embellishing thread is acceptable. Choose the option that gives you the effect *you* want.

The stitches I most commonly use are:

Blanket Stitch

Pin or baste the appliqué piece in place, then stitch. Be sure to catch both the appliqué and the background layers of fabric with each stitch.

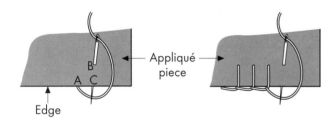

Keep your stitches loose. If you pull too tight, the outside thread or segment of the outline will disappear under the appliqué. Try to keep your stitches in uniform proportions throughout the piece. If you begin by making your stitches tall and close, keep that same proportion on a smaller appliqué piece.

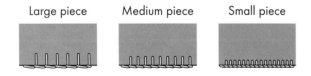

Here are two ways to group your blanket stitches on narrow or skinny pieces.

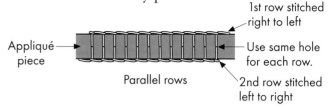

Tack corner stitches in place as you sew, or try many stitches grouped close together at a corner. Many stitches close together tend to lie flatter than an isolated stitch.

Group many stitches together at a corner.

Chain Stitch

Use a small stitch to hold the chain in place when changing directions.

French Knot

Lazy Daisy

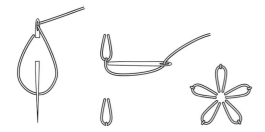

Feather Stitch

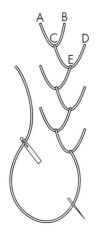

1. Bring the needle up at A, then down at B, forming a U-shape.
2. Bring the needle back up at C to form the "catch," then down at D, once again forming a U-shape.
3. Bring the needle back up at E to catch the U. Continue working to the left and right in this manner.

Backstitch

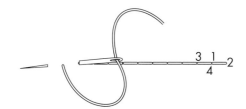

Herringbone Stitch

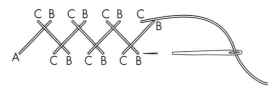

1. Bring the needle up at A and cross the seam at an angle. With the needle held parallel to the seam and pointing toward A, take a small stitch from B to C.
2. Return to the opposite side of the seam line in the same manner. Continue to the end of the seam.

Cross-stitch and Star Stitch

Running Stitch

This is what I use for my quilting stitch. It is big, bright, and bold.

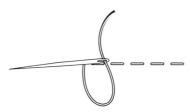

COTTON TECHNIQUES
Mini-Fuse

Prewash all cotton. Trace the pattern onto the top side (smooth paper side) of lightweight fusible web. The finished appliqué piece will be the reverse of what you trace. If you want an animal to face in a certain direction, *trace it facing in the opposite direction.* Trace all letters backward when using the mini-fuse technique.

In the monkey pattern and in some letters of the alphabet (such as R), you will need to cut out a small area inside the pattern.

1. Trace and leave a generous border of about ½" around each traced pattern.

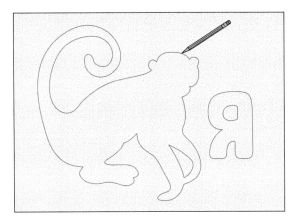

Trace on smooth side of fusible web.

2. Cut out the web from the center of the figure ⅛" inside the traced line, leaving a ⅛"-wide border all around the edge. Also leave a ⅛"-wide border around the inside of any cutout areas. Connect the inner border to the outer one by means of "bridges" so that the inner cutout border does not become separated from the outer border.

Bridge

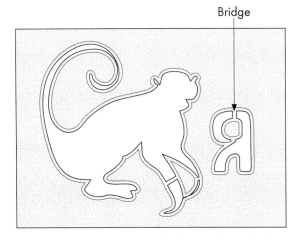

Remove inside area, leaving bridges and ⅛" border.

I find that a ⅛" border works well with the blanket stitch I sew. If your blanket stitch is larger, you can cut a more generous border. I don't recommend going any smaller than ⅛".

3. Press the fusible web to the wrong side of the cotton fabric. (This is when the need for the gener-

ous ½" of web around the traced figure becomes obvious. The web holds the shape of the appliqué pattern piece so it isn't distorted when fused in place.)

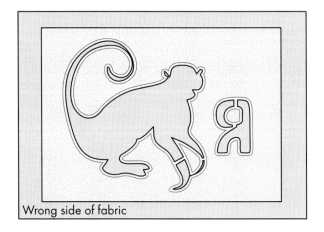

Wrong side of fabric

4. Cut out the cotton appliqué piece on the traced line. Remove the paper backing and position on the background fabric.

Wrong side

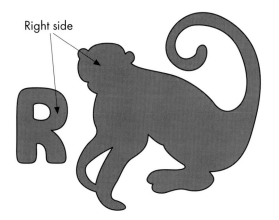

Right side

Ready to fuse in place

5. Do not fuse until all appliqué pieces are in place. This technique works for any size appliqué piece.

Cotton Tongue Borders

One of the most widely recognized characteristics of a penny rug is its tongue border. You can make a tongue border in wool, felt, or cotton, but cotton requires a little extra work.

1. Rotary cut cotton squares or rectangles according to the project instructions. With right sides together, pair up tongue front fabric with tongue back fabric.

Place 2 cotton rectangles
right sides together.

2. Cut rounded corners at one end of each pair. You can cut freehand or use a pattern.

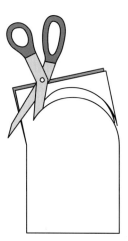

Cut freehand or
pin pattern in place.

3. Sew a double seam around the long curved edge of each tongue pair, using a ¼"-wide seam allowance. Trim close to the seam lines.

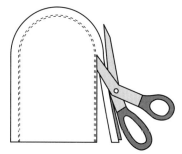

Double stitch a ¼"-wide seam allowance;
trim close to stitches.

4. Turn the tongues right side out and press.

NOTE: Cotton tongue borders require more than twice as much fabric as wool or felt tongue borders because you need twice as many tongue pieces and you must add a ¼"-wide seam allowance to each. Keep this in mind if you are converting a wool or felt pattern to cotton.

Quilt Bindings

I use cotton as my binding fabric no matter what fabric the quilt is made from. I like the weight of the fabric and the wide range of colors and patterns available in cotton.

Making the Binding

1. For a single-layer binding, use 1¼"-wide cotton strips. To make straight-grain binding, cut strips across the width of the fabric from selvage to selvage. Stitch the strips together, end to end, to make one continuous strip of binding. If you are binding curves, the strips need to be cut on the bias. To make bias-grain binding, I frequently use fat quarters (18" x 22"). Press the fabric, making sure the edges are on the straight grain (the threads that run parallel to the cut edge). Fold over one corner of the fabric diagonally to find the "true

bias" (the line that runs at a 45° angle to the straight grain).

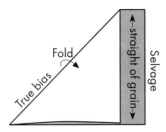

2. Cut along the fold line, then use it as a guide to rotary cut the number of 1¼"-wide strips needed to bind the quilt.

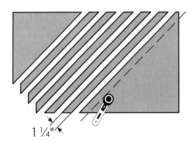

3. Stitch the pieces together as shown to make one continuous bias strip. Press the seams open.

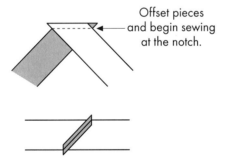

Sewing the Binding to the Quilt

1. With right sides together, line up the raw edges of the binding and the quilt top. Fold the beginning of the binding back ½" over itself and pin in place as shown. Using a ¼"-wide seam allowance, stitch along one side of the quilt, stop-

ping ¼" from the edge. Backstitch and clip the threads.

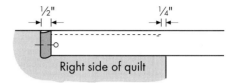

2. Remove the quilt from the machine. Fold the binding away from the quilt, perpendicular to the edge you just stitched, then fold it back down along the next edge to be stitched.

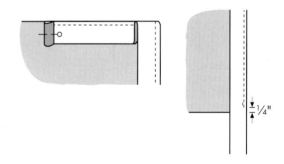

3. Starting at the top, stitch down the next side; stop ¼" from the next edge. Backstitch.

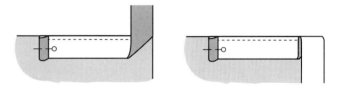

4. Repeat the corner turns. After you have stitched the binding to the quilt all the way around, overlap the binding about ¼" over the fold at the beginning. Trim off the extra binding, then finish stitching the binding to the quilt.

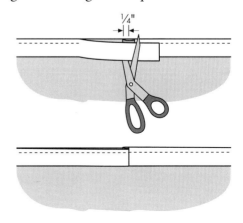

5. Turn the binding over to the back of the quilt and fold under ¼" along the raw edge. Pin and slipstitch in place. This hem will cover the machine stitching, and the corners will form folded miters.

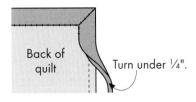

Back of quilt   Turn under ¼".

Fabric Marking Pens

Fabric markers of many colors and sizes are widely available. Using markers is a wonderful alternative to embroidering the animal details, such as eyes, ears, tails, or saddles. You can use them to shade or highlight an area or simply to sign and date your work. I find that markers work best on lighter colors of cotton. I occasionally use metallic paint markers on wool or felt. Always test on a scrap first.

WOOL AND FELT TECHNIQUES

Decorative Rotary Cutters

The patterned rotary blades made for fabric are perfect for felt because the crisp edge won't unravel or fray. You can attach the felt with embroidery stitches on top instead of covering every edge with stitches.

Embellishments

Sequins, beads, fringe, and buttons are just a few of the embellishments you can add to your projects. If you can attach it to your project and you like it, it's right! Silk ribbon is a delight to sew on wool. Embroidery floss, perle cotton, and crewel yarns are easy to work with on wool or felt.

Transferring Patterns

There are two ways to transfer the patterns that begin on page 41.

Method 1: For simple shapes that will be used only once or twice, I recommend using tracing paper to make templates. Trace the pattern onto tracing paper, cut out the pattern, then pin it to the wool or felt. Cut out the fabric. Do not add seam allowances to the paper, wool, or felt appliqué pieces.

Don't try to cut the paper and the fabric at the same time. Your scissors won't like it, and the edges of both the paper and the fabric will be ragged. Blanket stitches will not hide poorly cut edges.

Method 2: For pattern pieces that are highly detailed or that will be used many times, I recommend using a lightweight, nonfusible interfacing for the template. Lightweight interfacing is soft and flexible, so it is easy to work around when pinned to the background fabric. Trace the pattern from the book directly onto the interfacing. Cut out the interfacing and use it instead of a paper pattern. This is the best technique for making the "Peacock Pincushion" shown on page 36.

Wool and Felt Tongue Borders

Wool or felt tongue borders need only one-half the amount of fabric that a cotton tongue border needs. Keep this in mind if you are converting a cotton pattern to wool or felt. There are two ways to cut out tongue and penny shapes from wool or felt. The first is to use a paper or lightweight interfacing pattern pinned to the wool or felt.

The second way is what I refer to throughout this book as "the freehand method." Using a rotary cutter, cut squares or rectangles to the size given in the project instructions. To make a penny circle, use scissors to round off the corners of each square.

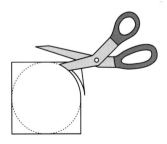

To make tongue shapes, round off two corners at the short end of a rectangle.

For wool, use blanket stitches to finish the rounded edge.

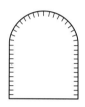

Felt edges can be left plain, finished with a blanket stitch, or given a decorative edge with pinking or scalloping shears.

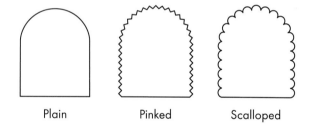

Plain   Pinked   Scalloped

SIGNING YOUR WORK

No project is complete without initials and a date (at the very least) appearing somewhere. How I wish ancestors on both my side and my husband's side of the family had left at least that much of a clue on their quilts and embroideries. I use the chain stitch to add my initials and date on the front of each completed piece.

A more detailed history can be included on the back of a piece by using a fine-tipped fabric pen on smooth fabric. Don't leave your descendants guessing.

Tools and Supplies

- Paper scissors
- Fabric scissors
- Pinking or scalloping shears
- Lightweight fusible web
- Rotary cutter with straight and decorative cutting edges
- Embroidery floss
- #8 crewel needles (or whatever works with the thread you choose)
- Straight pins, ¾" to 1"
- Tracing paper or lightweight interfacing
- Thin batting (such as a batting made for wearables)
- Cutting mat
- Acrylic ruler for cutting guide
- Sewing machine
- Pencil
- Fabric markers
- All-purpose sewing thread

Rita and Sue Pillow

Finished pillow size (including tongue border): 23" x 23"
Color photo on page 29

Rita and Sue are two very silly birds. They were also the first animals designed for Folk Art Animals. *Images of birds are found in the folk art of all cultures. This pillow is the perfect opportunity to dust off your pinking shears or to try the new rotary-cutting blades with decorative edges.*

Materials

This pillow can be made in any fabric. The example shown and the instructions given are for felt, but they also apply to wool. To make the pillow in cotton, you will need a little more than twice as much fabric for the tongue border.

- 1 piece *each* of yellow, pale green, hot pink, red, and blue felt, each 9" x 12", for pennies and birds
- 2 pieces *each* of purple, bright green, and navy blue felt, each 9" x 12", for tongue border
- 19" x 19" piece of background fabric
- 19" x 19" piece of backing fabric
- Embroidery floss
- Polyester stuffing

Cutting

Using the cutting diagrams on page 18, cut squares and rectangles for the pennies and tongues. Cut out the pennies and tongues using the templates on pages 41 and 42, or cut freehand as described on page 15.

Using the templates on pages 50 and 57, cut out the Rita and Sue appliqué pieces.

Using a wavy-edged rotary blade, cut:

- 4 bright green strips of felt, each ¼" x 5", with a wavy edge on both sides of the strip.
- 4 navy blue strips, each ¾" x 9", with a wavy edge on one side and a straight edge on the other.
- 2 red and 2 bright green strips, each 1¼" x 9", with a wavy edge on one side and a straight edge on the other.

Assembly

1. Make the 16 penny stacks as shown. Attach the smallest (top) penny to the medium-size and large pennies with a simple star stitch (page 11) through the center of all 3 layers.

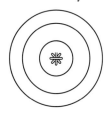

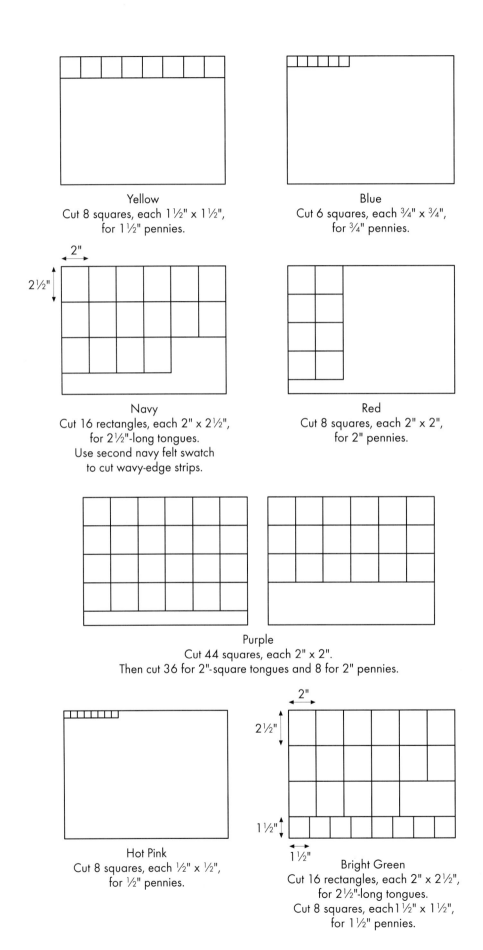

Yellow
Cut 8 squares, each 1½" x 1½",
for 1½" pennies.

Blue
Cut 6 squares, each ¾" x ¾",
for ¾" pennies.

Navy
Cut 16 rectangles, each 2" x 2½",
for 2½"-long tongues.
Use second navy felt swatch
to cut wavy-edge strips.

Red
Cut 8 squares, each 2" x 2",
for 2" pennies.

Purple
Cut 44 squares, each 2" x 2".
Then cut 36 for 2"-square tongues and 8 for 2" pennies.

Hot Pink
Cut 8 squares, each ½" x ½",
for ½" pennies.

Bright Green
Cut 16 rectangles, each 2" x 2½",
for 2½"-long tongues.
Cut 8 squares, each 1½" x 1½",
for 1½" pennies.

2. Make the decorative diagonal trims. Center 1 navy blue strip on each of the bright green and red strips. Blanket stitch (page 10) them together along the straight edge as shown.

Navy blue
Bright green

3. Arrange the appliqué pieces on the background fabric, referring to the diagram for placement. To place the 4 corner strips, measure in 5" from each corner and pin the pieces in place. The strips will extend beyond the edges of the background. Place the same color pairs in opposite corners.

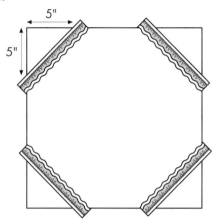

5"
5"

4. Use the chain stitch (page 10) to appliqué the corner strips and bright green center strips in place; then trim the corner strips even with the background fabric edges. Referring to the photo on page 29, use the chain stitch to appliqué Rita and Sue's feathers and Sue's legs.

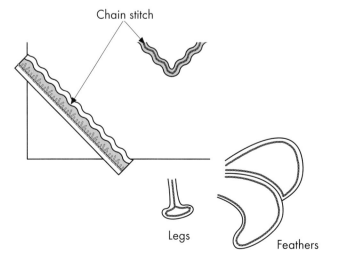

Chain stitch

Legs

Feathers

5. Appliqué the penny stacks to the background with a blanket-stitch variation. This is a good time to initial and date your work.

6. Arrange 9 purple border tongues along each edge of the pillow top. Leave a ⅜" space at each end. Baste them in place.

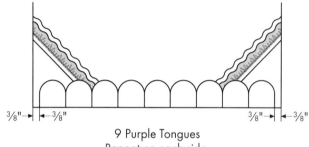

⅜" ⅜"   ⅜" ⅜"

9 Purple Tongues
Repeat on each side.
Tongues will overlap at corners.

7. Alternate navy blue and bright green border tongues along the edges, on top of the purple tongues, and baste them in place.

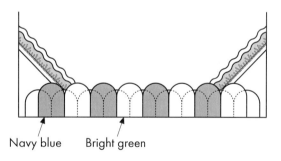

Navy blue   Bright green

8. With right sides together, sew the pillow top and backing together along all 4 edges, leaving an 8" opening for turning.

9. Turn right side out and stuff with polyester stuffing. Hand stitch the opening closed.

"Whatever You Are, Be a Good One" Pillow

Finished pillow size (including tongue border): 25" x 25"
Color photo on page 29

Materials

This pillow can be made in any fabric. The example shown and the instructions given are for felt, but they also apply to wool. To make the pillow in cotton, you will need at least twice as much fabric for the tongue border.

- 1 piece of yellow felt, 9" x 12"
- 3 pieces *each* of navy blue and bright green felt, each 9" x 12"
- 2 pieces of red felt, each 9" x 12"
- 4 or 5 assorted colors of felt scraps for leaves and pennies
- 20" x 20" piece of background fabric
- 20" x 20" piece of backing fabric
- Embroidery floss
- Polyester stuffing

Cutting

Using the cutting diagrams on page 21, cut pieces for the tongue border. Cut out the tongues using the templates on page 41, or freehand cut as described on page 15.

Using the templates indicated, cut:

- 17 pennies (1") (page 42)
- Proverb letters (pages 44–45)
- 19 assorted leaves, ⅞" and 1¾" long (page 42)
- 1 tree trunk, 9¼" long (page 47)
- 1 hilltop (page 48)
- 4 branches, each 5" long (page 47)
- 1 owl (page 58)

NOTE: If you make this pillow in cotton, be sure to trace the letters backward so they will read correctly after they are fused.

Assembly

1. Arrange the appliqué pieces on the background fabric, referring to the photo on page 29 for placement. Pin them in place.

2. Use the feather stitch to appliqué the tree trunk and branch; use the chain stitch for the leaves, and the star stitch for the pennies. Use the blanket stitch to appliqué the letters, owl, and hilltop. Embroider the owl.

3. Initial and date your work.

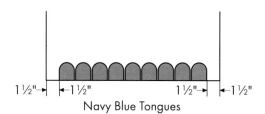

1½"→| |←1½"→| |←1½"→| |←1½"

Navy Blue Tongues

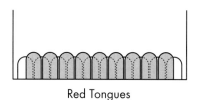

Bright Green Tongues

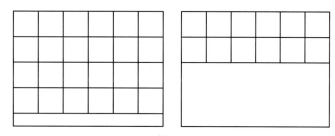

Red Tongues

4. Arrange 9 navy blue, 10 bright green, and 9 red tongues along each edge of the pillow top as shown at left; baste in place.

5. With right sides together, sew the pillow top and backing together along all 4 edges, leaving an 8" opening for turning.

6. Turn right side out and stuff with polyester stuffing. Hand stitch the opening closed.

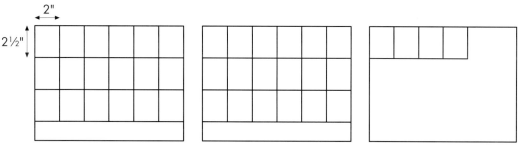

Navy
Cut 36 squares, each 2" x 2", for 2"-square tongues.

2"

2½"

Green
Cut 40 rectangles, each 2" x 2½", for 2½"-long tongues.

2"

3"

Red
Cut 36 rectangles, each 2" x 3", for 3"-long tongues.

Peacock Pincushion

Finished pillow size: 8½" x 8½"
Color photo on page 36

This little pillow is inspired by one of the many doodads the Victorians were so good at creating. Straight pins were precious at one time. A whole pincushion filled with pins was often presented to a woman as a gift. The arrangements of the pins could be simple or elaborate, depending on how many pins the giver could afford to present.

Warning: This is not a toy. Keep away from infants and small children.

Materials

This pincushion can be made in any solid-colored fabric.

- 2 squares, each 9" x 9", of fabric for cushion top and bottom
- Polyester stuffing
- 1 yd. decorative trim or braid
- 1 package of 1" silver straight pins (approximately 250)
- 1 package of 1" gold straight pins (approximately 200)
- Fabric markers or pens
- *Optional:* lightweight interfacing for pattern

Assembly

1. With right sides together, sew the cushion front and back together along all 4 edges, leaving a small opening for turning.

2. Turn the cushion right sides out and stuff with polyester stuffing. Hand stitch the opening closed.

3. Hand stitch decorative braid along the seam around the cushion, turning under edges where they meet.

4. Trace the hilltop (page 48) and peacock (page 54) templates on thin paper or lightweight interfacing. Cut out the patterns just inside the outline.

5. Center the pattern pieces on top of the cushion. Hold them in place with a few pins stuck through the paper or interfacing. These will not be part of the design, but will be removed once the decorative pins are in place.

6. Outline the peacock with silver pins. Place the pins right next to the pattern edge. The heads of the pins may overlap the pattern. It is easy to slip the pattern out from under them. Try to stick the pins in straight down, not at funny angles, and space them evenly. If all of the pins are straight, the heads of the pins will lie flat against the top of the cushion.

7. Insert pins in the cutaway areas of the peacock body.

8. Remove the pattern pieces. Referring to the photo and template, add gold pins for feathers. Feel free to add more borders or designs.

9. Using a fabric marker or pen, sign and date the back of your pincushion.

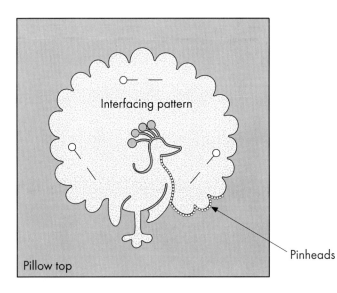

Interfacing pattern

Pinheads

Pillow top

The Great Pyramid Table Runner

Finished table runner size: 17¾" x 78" (for 42" x 60" table)
Color photo on page 30

You can custom design a runner to fit your table. Measure your table length and add 6" at each end for overhang. Start building the animal pyramid at the table edge. If your table is large, you may need more squares for the center; for a small table, you will need fewer squares.

Materials

This table runner can be made in any fabric. The example shown and the instructions given are for toweling by the yard, but they also apply to felt and wool. With all of the beautiful homespun plaids, stripes, and prints now available, you will easily find a wonderful substitute if you can't find toweling by the yard. Remember to add seam allowances for cotton.

- 17¾" x 78" piece of toweling by the yard *or* several individual towels sewn together (either end to end or side by side) *or* checkered fabric, 18¾" x 78"
- 3 pieces of red felt, each 9" x 12"
- 1 piece of white felt, 9" x 12"
- Embroidery floss

Cutting

Use the templates indicated.
From the red felt, cut:

- 2 goose bodies (page 57), 2 cats (page 59), 2 sheep (page 51), 2 donkeys (page 54), 4 horses (page 61), and 4 ox bodies (page 56)
- 25 squares, each 1½" x 1½"

From the white felt, cut:

- goose legs and wings (page 57), sheep flowers (page 43), donkey heart (page 54), horse saddle (page 61), and ox horns (page 56)

Assembly

1. Cut toweling to the desired length. Fringe 1" at each short end. Machine stitch with a straight stitch across the base of the fringe at each end.

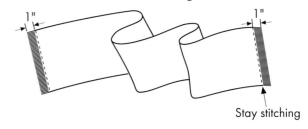

Stay stitching

2. Arrange all appliqué pieces on the table-runner fabric. Pin in place.

3. Blanket stitch all pieces to the background and embroider the details as shown (see "Embroidery Stitches" on page 10).

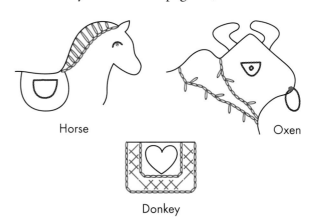

Horse

Oxen

Donkey

4. Sign and date your work.

Barnyard Parade

Finished quilt size: 17" x 27"
Color photo on page 30

A parade of animals is a delightful subject to play with. Feel free to add balloons, streamers, or even fire-works if that is what your parade wants! All of the animals in the book could be arranged for a whimsical border around the cornice of a child's room. Arranged vertically, the animals could decorate a door frame to measure a child's growth. Two pillow shams placed side by side could showcase parts of the same parade, or the border of a quilt could be decorated with these celebrating critters.

Materials

This wall hanging can be made in any fabric. The example shown and the instructions given are for prewashed felt, but they also apply to wool and cotton.

- 12 pieces, each 9" x 12", of 6 different felt colors for appliqué pieces and pennies
- 17" x 27" piece of background fabric
- 17" x 27" piece of cotton backing fabric
- 1¼"-wide strips for 98" of binding
- Embroidery floss

Cutting

Use the templates indicated.

From the assorted colors of felt, cut:

- Harnesses, flags, and beanie propeller hat (page 43); chicks in a wagon and hay wagon (page 48); 1 sheep (page 51); 1 pig (page 53); 1 goose (page 57); and 1 rooster (page 58)

From the remaining assorted colors of felt, cut:

- 47 large (2") pennies (page 42)
- 47 medium (1¼") pennies (page 42)

Assembly

1. Referring to the photo on page 30, arrange all appliqué pieces on the background. It is important to have everything in place so the goose's flag and beanie propeller hat fill the area of the one missing penny. Pin or baste all pieces in place.

2. Using a blanket stitch, appliqué the pieces to the background. Embroider the details as shown.

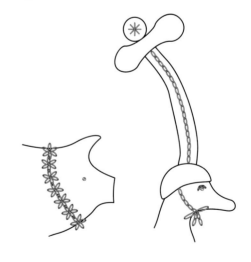

3. Add the backing fabric and bind the two pieces together (see "Quilt Bindings" on page 13).

4. Sign and date your quilt.

Laplander Squares

Finished quilt size: 23" x 23"
Color photo on page 31

From the beginning, this quilt had a mind of its own and was never really interested in my personal vision. I finally decided to let the quilt evolve in its own way. I will admit to being very tired of the quilt when it was finally finished, but now I love the look of all the embroidery. It might have been easier to use a print fabric for sashing and forgo all of the handwork, but the texture would have been different and not as interesting.

Materials

This quilt can be made in any fabric. The example shown and the instructions given are for cotton.

- 1 fat quarter of white background fabric
- ½ yd. of red fabric for animal appliqués, sashing, and border
- ½ yd. of backing fabric
- 1 fat quarter of navy blue fabric for binding
- Thin batting
- Embroidery floss in navy blue, green, gold, red, and white
- Lightweight fusible web
- 1 index card
- Embroidery hoop

Cutting

Before cutting the animal appliqué pieces, read "Mini-Fuse" on page 11.

From the white background fabric, cut:

- 9 squares, each 5½" x 5½"

From the red fabric, cut:

- 2 female reindeer and 2 reversed (page 53)
- 1 polar bear and 1 reversed (page 60)
- 2 male reindeer and 2 reversed (page 60)
- 6 strips, each 2½" x 5½", for sashing
- 4 strips, each 2½" x 19½", for sashing and border
- 2 strips, each 2½" x 23½", for border

From the fat quarter of navy blue fabric, cut:

- 1¼"-wide strips for 96" of binding

Assembly

1. Center 1 animal on each background square. Fuse in place and appliqué with the blanket stitch (page 10). Embroider the details as shown.

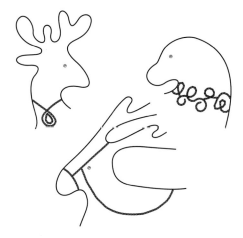

2. Assemble the blocks and sashing as shown.

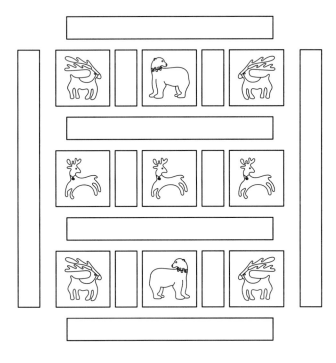

3. Using the index card, make an embroidery guide from the template on page 42. Mark the embroidery lines on the quilt top.

4. Chain stitch (page 10) on the marked lines with 2 strands of navy blue embroidery floss.

5. Work a line of herringbone stitches (page 11) ⅛" inside the chain-stitched line, using 2 strands of navy blue floss.

6. Add 3 lazy daisy stitches (page 11) with 2 strands of green floss at each corner of the herringbone stitching, as shown on page 31.

7. Layer the quilt top with batting and backing. Pin or baste the layers together. With 1 strand of navy blue floss, echo quilt around each animal within the block.

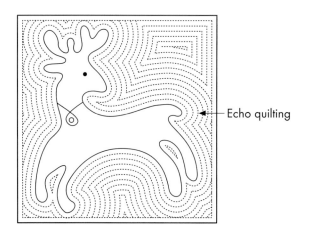
Echo quilting

8. Using a single strand of embroidery floss, echo quilt alternate squares in green and white.

9. Using a single strand of white embroidery floss, quilt 1 row outside the navy blue chain stitching.

10. Using a strand of gold embroidery floss, echo quilt outside the white row of quilting.

11. Using 2 strands of gold floss, chain stitch through all 3 layers, next to the line of gold quilting. Echo quilt the remaining border area with a single strand of red floss.

12. Bind the quilt with cotton strips (page 13).

13. Sign and date your quilt.

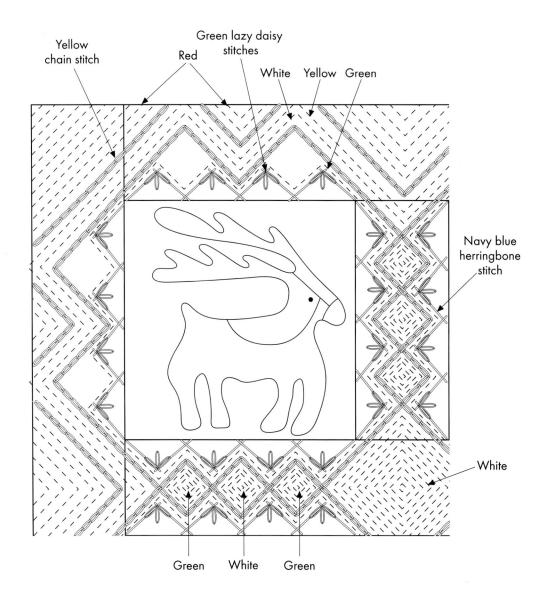

Stitch Guide

Gallery

RITA AND SUE PILLOW
by Janet Carija Brandt, 1997, Indianapolis,
Indiana, 23" x 23". This bold decorative
pillow is easy to make with wool felt.

WHATEVER YOU ARE PILLOW
by Janet Carija Brandt, 1997, Indianapolis,
Indiana, 25" x 25". This felt pillow is a
great opportunity to play with
decorative-edge scissors.

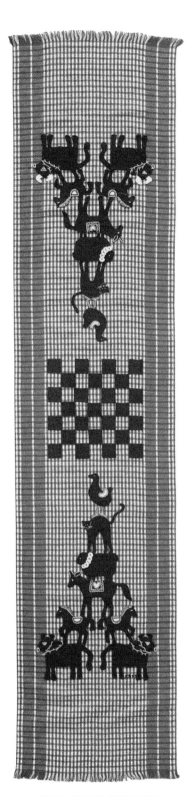

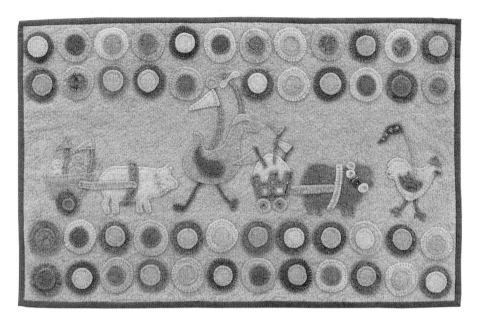

BARNYARD PARADE
by Janet Carija Brandt, 1997, Indianapolis, Indiana, 17" x 27".
This soft-appearing quilt was inspired by penny rugs.

THE GREAT PYRAMID
TABLE RUNNER
by Janet Carija Brandt, 1997,
Indianapolis, Indiana, 17¾" x 78".
Try toweling by the yard for this
fun table runner.

SAVE THE BEARS
by Lucy Brown and Milly Churbuck, 1997, Ames, Iowa, 21" x 17".
Here, the penny motif has become flowers.

LAPLANDER SQUARES
by Janet Carija Brandt, 1997,
Indianapolis, Indiana, 23" x 23".
Northern animals appear in
traditional Laplander colors.

LANTERNS IN THE NIGHT
by Janet Carija Brandt, 1997,
Indianapolis, Indiana,
25" x 31½". Do the
animals party late into
the jungle night?

LITTLE LAMB
by Debra Haggard, 1997, Greenwood, Indiana,
15½" x 14". The lamb's fluffy coat is a
meandering chain stitch.

THE LORD GOD MADE THEM ALL
by Janet Carija Brandt, 1997, Indianapolis, Indiana, 41½" x 29½". This quilt was also inspired by
traditional penny-rug design. Notice how well cotton works for these designs.

REDWORK SAMPLER
by Debby Eads, 1997, Indianapolis,
Indiana, 24½" x 29".
Folk animals of the world are worked
with a red stem stitch.

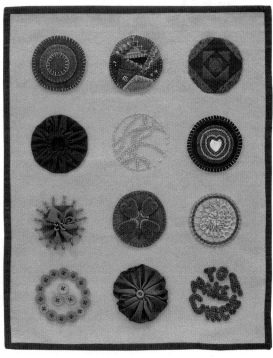

TO MAKE A CIRCLE
by Janet Carija Brandt, 1996, Indianapolis,
Indiana, 15" x 18". How many ways can you
use circles in a penny rug? Here are a few
ideas to get you started.

AUTUMN NIGHT
by Debra Haggard, 1997, Greenwood, Indiana, 23" x 17½". Deb turned her pennies into pumpkins.

EASTER PARADE
by Debra Haggard, 1997, Greenwood, Indiana, 30½" x 15½". This red hen is a proud mom indeed.

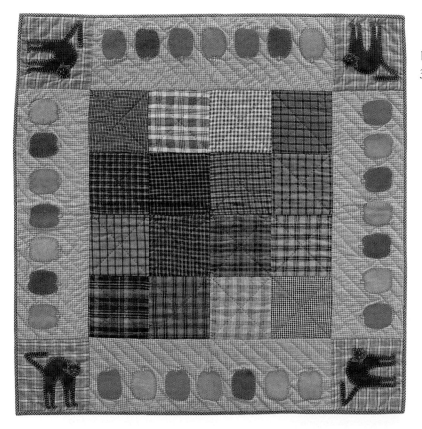

CATS ON A HOT PLAID QUILT
by Debby Eads, 1997, Indianapolis, Indiana,
32" x 32". Debby combined her collection of
cats and pumpkins with a wonderful
collection of homespun plaids.

TWO BY TWO
by Little Quilts (Alice Berg, Sylvia Johnson, and
Mary Ellen Von Holt), 1997, Marietta, Georgia,
27" x 30". Little Quilts' "Noah's Ark" pattern has
been embellished with
folk art animals and raindrops.

PEACOCK PINCUSHION
by Janet Carija Brandt, 1997, Indianapolis, Indiana,
8½" x 8½". Any animal would work well for this
charming pillow.

LION PINCUSHION
by Janet Carija Brandt, 1997, Indianapolis,
Indiana, 8½" x 8½".

SHEEP DREAMS
by Betsy Harris, 1997, Zionsville, Indiana, 19" x 14½". You'd never have trouble falling asleep
if you had these pretty sheep to count.

The Lord God Made Them All

Finished quilt size: 29½" x 41½"
Color photo on page 32

The quote "All things bright and beautiful, all creatures great and small, all things wise and wonderful, the Lord God made them all," from Cecil Frances Alexander, inspired this quilt. Each of the twenty-five folk art animal designs is here. This quilt, with its colorful tongue border, is all cotton. All of the animal details are added with fabric markers. Embroidery would be equally effective. You can use this quilt as a wall hanging, lap robe, or baby blanket.

Materials

This quilt can be made from any fabric. Fabric measurements given are for prewashed cotton. If you use wool or felt, you will need only half as much for the tongue border.

- 1 yd. yellow background fabric
- 1 fat quarter *each* of blue, yellow-orange, orange-red, green, and purple fabric
- 1 yd. red fabric for border and animals
- 1 yd. light green backing fabric
- Lightweight fusible web
- Fabric markers
- Embroidery floss in coordinating colors
- Thin batting

Cutting

Before cutting the cotton appliqué pieces, read "Mini-Fuse" on page 11.

From the yellow background fabric, cut:

- Background, 24½" x 36½"
- 1½"-wide strips for 150" of binding

From the 5 assorted colors, cut:

- 1 of each animal desired (for ideas, see photo on page 32)
- 19 large (1½") pennies and approximately 50 small (¾") pennies
- Letters

N O T E : Remember to trace the letters backward when you are using the mini-fuse technique.

- 128 rectangles, each 2¼" x 2¼", for tongues

From the red fabric, cut:

- 2 strips, each 3" x 29½"
- 2 strips, each 3" x 36½"

From the light green backing fabric, cut:

- 1 piece, 29½" x 41½"

Assembly

1. Prepare the background by basting a guide-line 2¾" inside each edge.

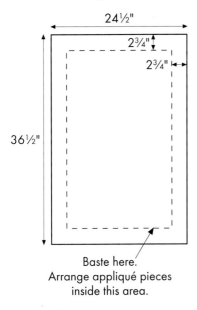

Baste here.
Arrange appliqué pieces
inside this area.

2. Remove the paper backing from the animals and arrange them on the background fabric inside the basted lines.

3. Randomly arrange pennies in spaces around the animals. In the quilt shown on page 32, some large pennies have small pennies in their centers; others do not. Save 3 small pennies for the letter border. Check your composition. When you are happy with the placement of all of the animals and pennies, fuse everything in place.

4. Blanket stitch each piece in place. Add necessary details, such as eyes, ears, tails, or strips, with fabric markers or embroidery stitches.

5. Arrange letters around the outside of the animal area. One small penny separates each phrase. Check placement, fuse, and appliqué letters, using the blanket stitch.

6. Prepare pieces for the cotton tongue border (see page 13). If you are making the quilt in wool or felt, cut out only half the number of tongue border pieces. Work the blanket stitch around the rounded edges of the wool or felt tongues. This is not necessary with the cotton pieces.

7. Arrange the tongues, right side down, around the quilt edges. Center 19 tongues on each long edge and 13 tongues on each short edge. Leave ⅜" at each corner. Tongues will temporarily overlap at corners. Baste in place.

8. Add the border pieces.

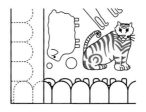

Add long borders on sides.

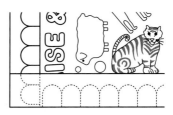

Add top and bottom borders.

9. Layer the quilt top, batting, and backing. Pin or baste the layers together. Contour quilt around each animal and around the tops of the tongue border.

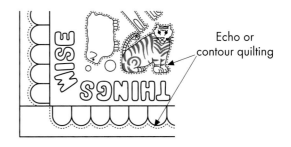

Echo or
contour quilting

10. Bind the quilt with cotton strips (page 13).

11. Sign and date your quilt.

Lanterns in the Night

Finished quilt size: 25" x 31½"
Color photo on page 31

Color is a very effective way to set a mood. For "Lanterns in the Night," dark, subdued colors help establish a nighttime mood, with paper lanterns casting a soft glow.

Materials

This penny rug can be made in any fabric. The example shown and instructions given are for wool and felt. Remember to buy more fabric for the tongues if you use cotton.

- 25" x 31½" piece of navy blue background fabric
- 25" x 31½" piece of backing fabric
- 12" x 18" piece of dark green fabric for camel
- 12" x 18" piece of medium green fabric for monkey
- 22" x 28" piece of dark brown fabric for elephant and trees
- 12" x 18" piece of medium brown fabric for giraffe
- 12" x 18" piece of light brown fabric for tiger
- 12" x 18" piece of dark gold fabric for lion
- 4" x 6" piece of white fabric for lanterns
- 4" x 6" piece of gold fabric for lantern pennies
- Gold embroidery floss
- 1 fat quarter of fabric for binding
- *Optional:* narrow ribbon

Cutting

Use the templates indicated. Lengthen or shorten the tree trunk template to the size needed.

From the dark green fabric, cut:

- 1 camel (page 55)

From the medium green fabric, cut:

- 1 monkey (page 59)

From the dark brown fabric, cut:

- 1 elephant (page 56)
- 2 tree trunks, each 10½" long (page 47)
- 2 tree trunks, each 8½" long (page 47)

From the medium brown fabric, cut:

- 1 giraffe (page 52)

From the light brown fabric, cut:

- 1 tiger (page 49)

From the dark gold fabric, cut:

- 1 lion (page 51)

From the white fabric, cut:

- 5 lanterns (page 42)

From the gold fabric, cut:

- 5 large (2") pennies (page 42)

From the remaining scraps, cut:

- 32 large (2") pennies (page 42)
- 48 small (1") pennies (page 42)
- 35 palm leaves in assorted 2" and 2½" sizes (page 42)
- 54 tongues, each 1¾" x 2" (page 41)

From the fat quarter, cut:

- 1¼"-wide strips for 115" of binding

Assembly

1. Assemble 32 penny stacks by securing one small penny to the center of each large penny with a blanket stitch (page 10).

2. Arrange all appliqué pieces on the background fabric, referring to the photo on page 31 for placement.

3. When you are satisfied with the arrangement, pin or baste the pieces in place. Blanket stitch each piece to the background fabric.

4. To help visualize the "ropes" that the lanterns and monkey are suspended from, pin a piece of narrow ribbon where you will chain stitch the ropes.

5. Add chain-stitched details to animals and tree trunks, using the markings on the patterns as a guide. Replace the ribbon ropes with chain stitches.

6. Echo quilt around each lantern penny, using 2 strands of gold embroidery floss to make them "shine."

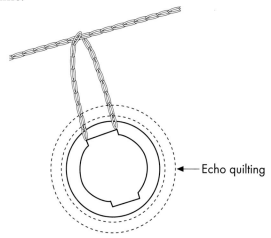

Echo quilting

7. Add backing fabric and bind the penny rug as you would a quilt (page 13).

8. Sign and date your penny rug.

Patterns and Templates

Patterns and templates may be copied, enlarged, or reduced for private use by the owner of this book.

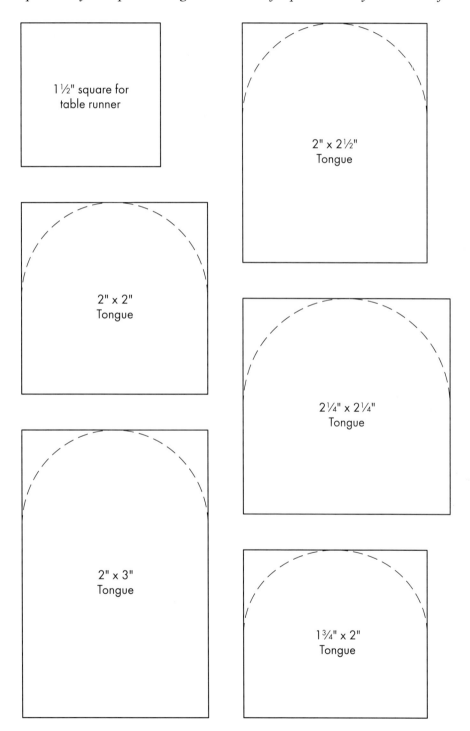

1½" square for table runner

2" x 2½" Tongue

2" x 2" Tongue

2¼" x 2¼" Tongue

2" x 3" Tongue

1¾" x 2" Tongue

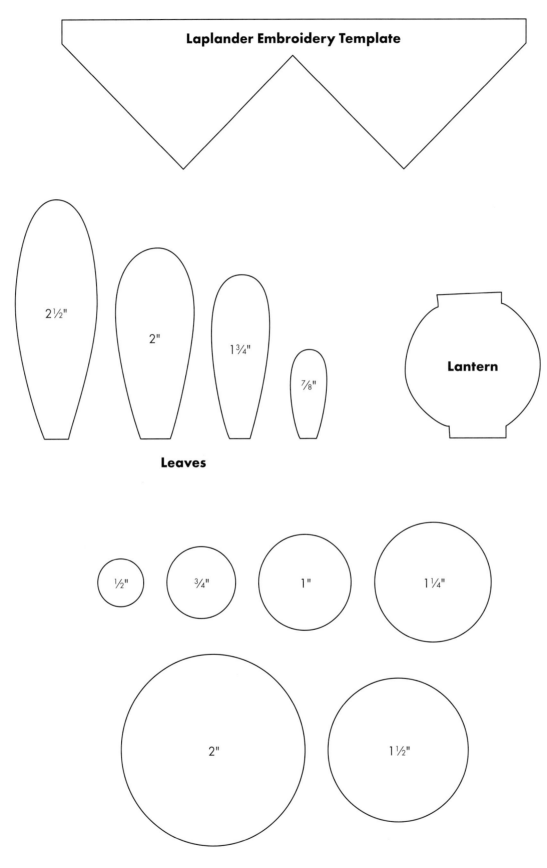

Laplander Embroidery Template

2½"

2"

1¾"

⅞"

Lantern

Leaves

½"

¾"

1"

1¼"

2"

1½"

Pennies

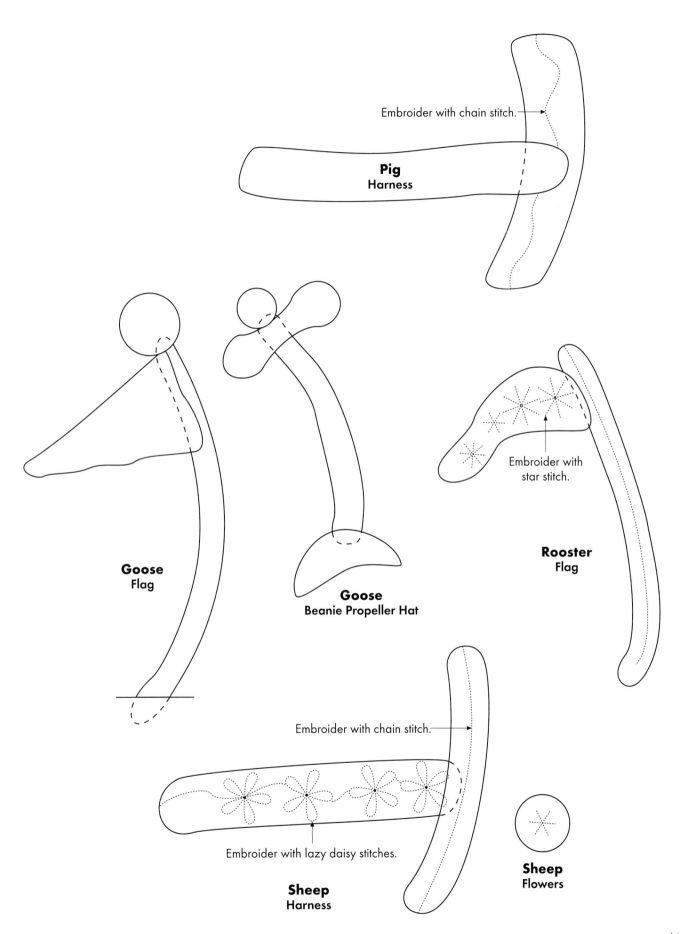

Embroider with chain stitch.

Pig
Harness

Goose
Flag

Goose
Beanie Propeller Hat

Embroider with
star stitch.

Rooster
Flag

Embroider with chain stitch.

Embroider with lazy daisy stitches.

Sheep
Harness

Sheep
Flowers

A B C D

E F G H I

J K L M

NOPQ
RSTUV
WXYZ

Note: Flip the 6 upside down for the 9.

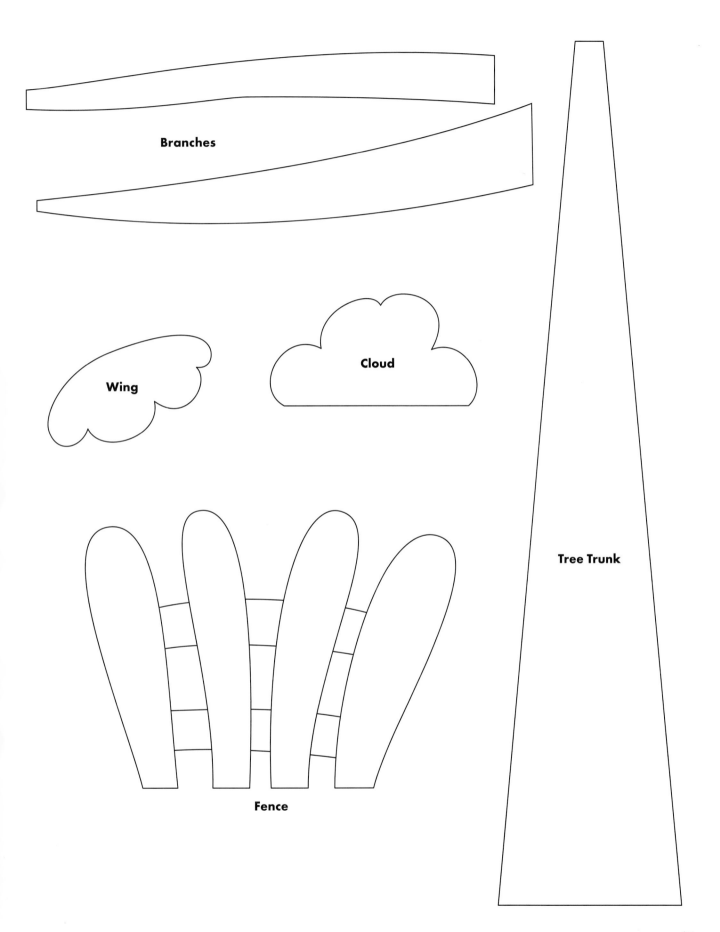

Branches

Wing

Cloud

Tree Trunk

Fence

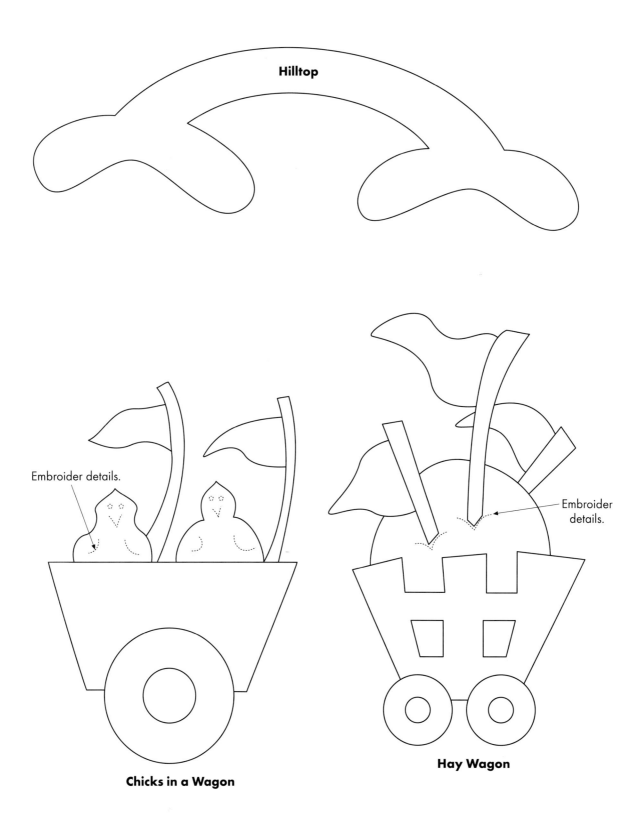

Hilltop

Embroider details.

Embroider details.

Chicks in a Wagon

Hay Wagon

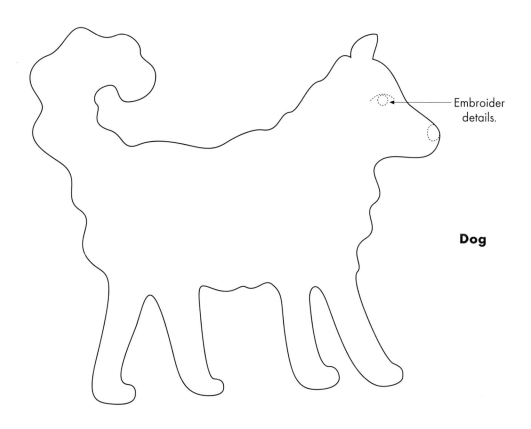

Embroider
details.

Dog

Embroider details.

Tiger

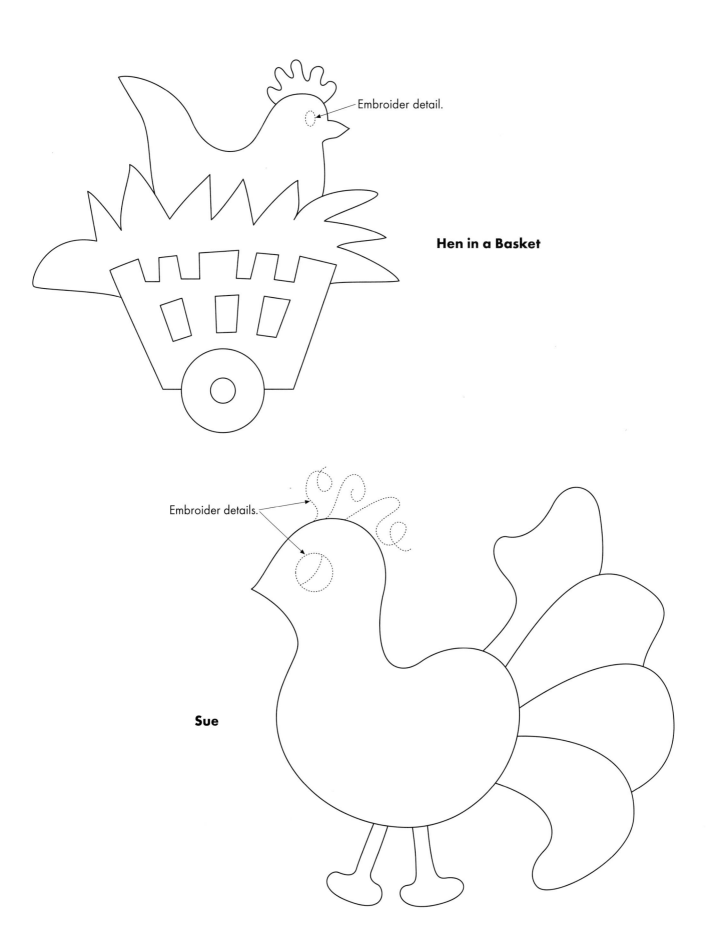

Embroider detail.

Hen in a Basket

Embroider details.

Sue

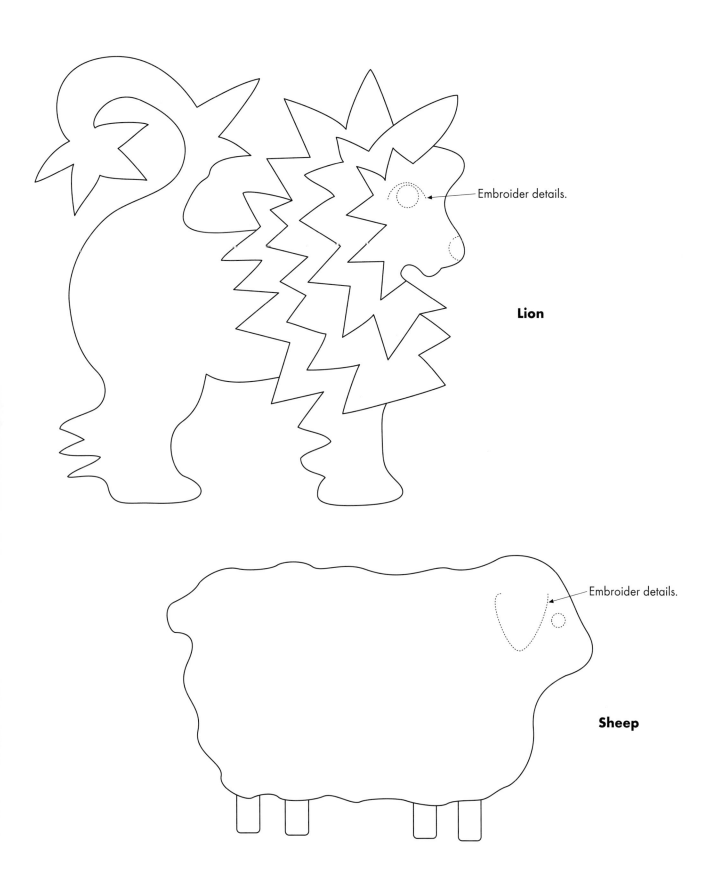

Embroider details.

Lion

Embroider details.

Sheep

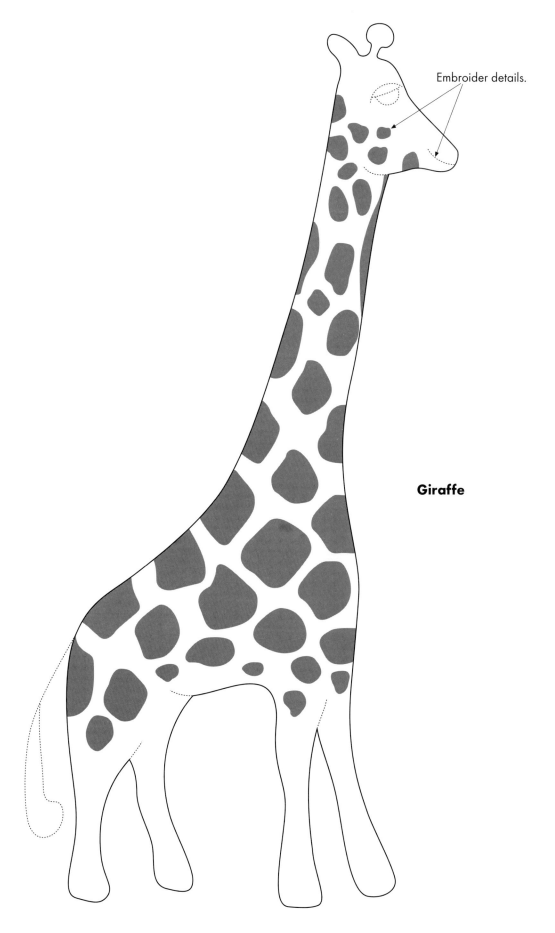

Embroider details.

Giraffe

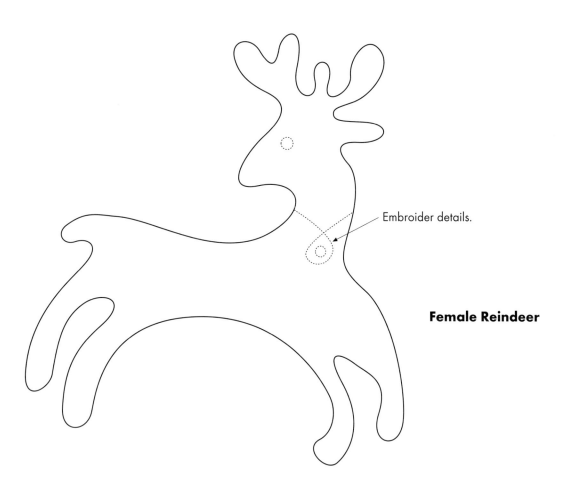

Embroider details.

Female Reindeer

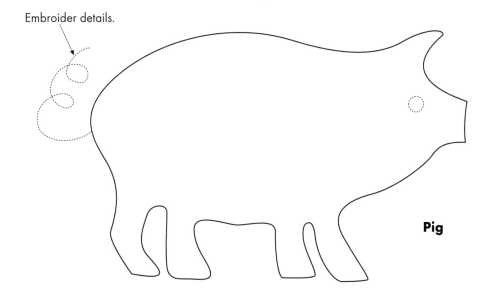

Embroider details.

Pig

Embroider details.

Peacock

Embroider details.

Donkey

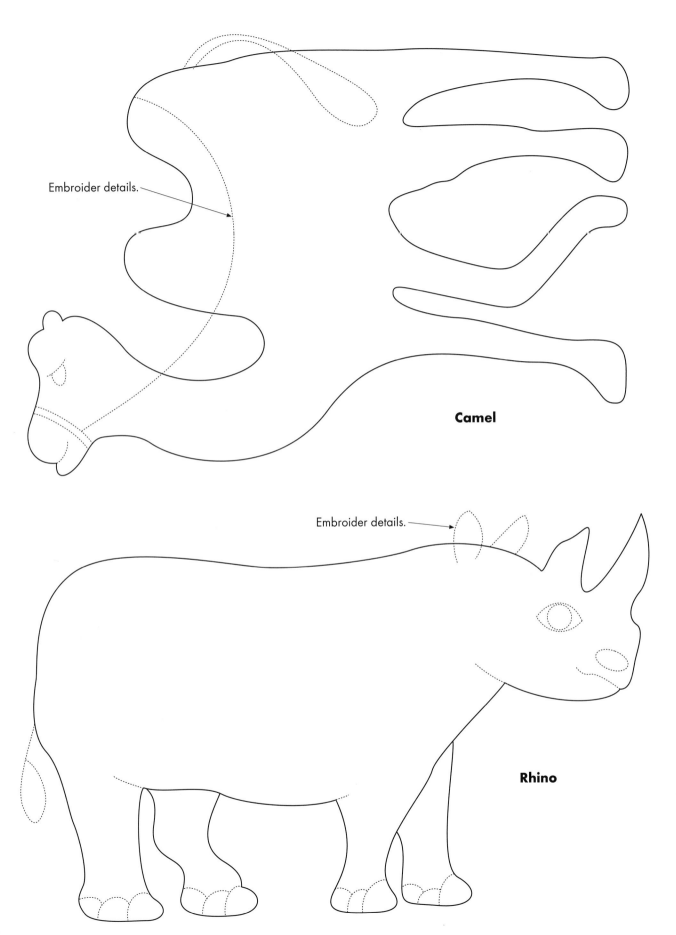

Embroider details.

Camel

Embroider details.

Rhino

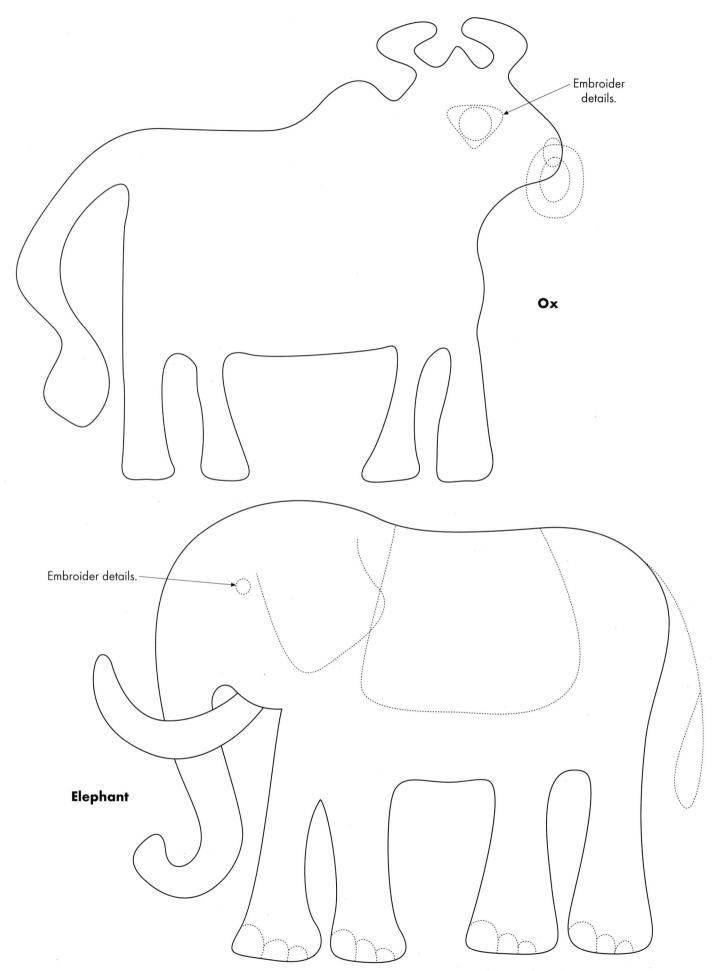

Embroider
details.

Ox

Embroider details.

Elephant

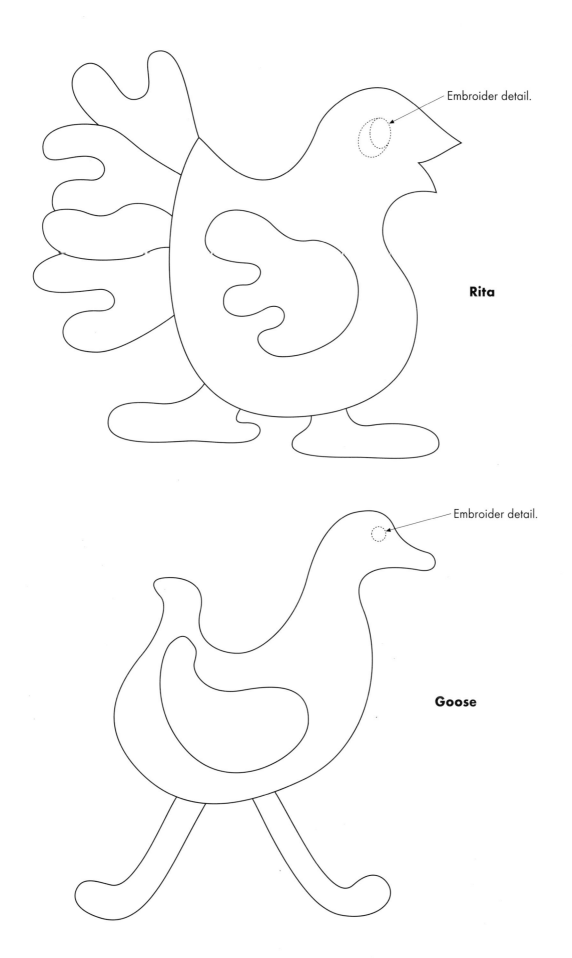

Embroider detail.

Rita

Embroider detail.

Goose

Embroider detail.

Rooster

Embroider details.

Owl

Embroider details.

Cat

Embroider details.

Monkey

Embroider details.

Male Reindeer

Embroider details.

Polar Bear

Embroider details.

Fox

Embroider details.

Horse

RESOURCES AND SUPPLIES

Wool
Kings Road
548 South Los Angeles Street
Los Angeles, CA 90013
1-800-433-1546

Felt
National Nonwovens
PO Box 150
Easthampton, MA 01027

Hand-Dyed Cotton
Country House Cottons
PO Box 375
Fayette, IA 52142

Embroidery Floss
The DMC Corporation
10 Port Kearny
South Kearny, NJ 07032-4688

ABOUT THE AUTHOR

FROM AN EARLY AGE, Janet Carija Brandt has been in love with all things tactile. She has done fashion display, illustration, and buying, along with graphic design and architectural modeling. She has hooked rugs, crocheted, and knit; sewn wearables, quilts, and dolls; and embroidered. Her work has been featured in the Fairfield Fashion Show, the *Fiberarts Design Book V*, and numerous magazines. Twice she was named an Outstanding Traditional American Craftsman by *Early American Life* magazine. She is also the author of *WOW! Wool-on-Wool Folk Art Quilts.*

Janet says she is still happily afflicted with "make-thing-itis" and feels blessed with a loving husband, two wonderful children, a roof over her head, and plenty of food on the table. "It just doesn't get any better."

THAT PATCHWORK PLACE TITLES:

AMERICA'S BEST-LOVED QUILT BOOKS®

All-Star Sampler • Roxanne Carter
Appliquilt® for Christmas • Tonee White
Appliquilt® to Go • Tonee White
Around the Block with Judy Hopkins
At Home with Quilts • Nancy J. Martin
Awash with Colour • Judy Turner
Baltimore Bouquets • Mimi Dietrich
Bargello Quilts • Marge Edie
*Basic Quiltmaking Techniques for Hand
    Appliqué* • Mimi Dietrich
Beyond Charm Quilts
    • Catherine L. McIntee & Tammy L. Porath
Blockbender Quilts • Margaret J. Miller
Block by Block • Beth Donaldson
Borders by Design • Paulette Peters
The Border Workbook • Janet Kime
The Cat's Meow • Janet Kime
Celebrate! with Little Quilts • Alice Berg,
    Mary Ellen Von Holt & Sylvia Johnson
Celebrating the Quilt
Class-Act Quilts
Classic Quilts with Precise Foundation Piecing
    • Tricia Lund & Judy Pollard
Color: The Quilter's Guide • Christine Barnes
Colourwash Quilts • Deirdre Amsden
Crazy but Pieceable • Hollie A. Milne
Crazy Rags • Deborah Brunner
Decorate with Quilts & Collections
    • Nancy J. Martin
Design Essentials: The Quilter's Guide
    • Lorraine Torrence
Design Your Own Quilts • Judy Hopkins
Down the Rotary Road with Judy Hopkins
Dress Daze • Judy Murrah
Dressed by the Best
The Easy Art of Appliqué
    • Mimi Dietrich & Roxi Eppler
Easy Machine Paper Piecing • Carol Doak
Easy Mix & Match Machine Paper Piecing
    • Carol Doak
Easy Paper-Pieced Keepsake Quilts
    • Carol Doak
Easy Paper-Pieced Miniatures
    • Carol Doak
Easy Reversible Vests • Carol Doak
Easy Seasonal Wall Quilts
    • Deborah J. Moffett-Hall
Easy Star Sampler • Roxanne Carter
A Fine Finish • Cody Mazuran
Folk Art Animals • Janet Carija Brandt
Folk Art Quilts • Sandy Bonsib
Freedom in Design • Mia Rozmyn
From a Quilter's Garden • Gabrielle Swain
Go Wild with Quilts • Margaret Rolfe
Go Wild with Quilts—Again! • Margaret Rolfe
Great Expectations • Karey Bresenhan
    with Alice Kish & Gay E. McFarland
Hand-Dyed Fabric Made Easy
    • Adriene Buffington
Happy Endings • Mimi Dietrich
Honoring the Seasons • Takako Onoyama
Interlacing Borders • Donna Hussain
Jacket Jazz • Judy Murrah
Jacket Jazz Encore • Judy Murrah

The Joy of Quilting
    • Joan Hanson & Mary Hickey
Kids Can Quilt • Barbara J. Eikmeier
Life in the Country with Country Threads
    • Mary Tendall & Connie Tesene
Little Quilts • Alice Berg, Mary Ellen Von Holt &
    Sylvia Johnson
Lively Little Logs • Donna McConnell
Living with Little Quilts • Alice Berg,
    Mary Ellen Von Holt & Sylvia Johnson
The Log Cabin Design Workbook
    • Christal Carter
Lora & Company • Lora Rocke
Loving Stitches • Jeana Kimball
*Machine Needlelace and Other
    Embellishment Techniques* • Judy Simmons
Machine Quilting Made Easy • Maurine Noble
Machine Quilting with Decorative Threads
    • Maurine Noble & Elizabeth Hendricks
*Magic Base Blocks for Unlimited Quilt
    Designs* • Patty Barney & Cooky Schock
Make Room for Quilts (revised)
    • Nancy J. Martin
Miniature Baltimore Album Quilts
    • Jenifer Buechel
More Jazz from Judy Murrah
More Quilts for Baby • Ursula Reikes
More Strip-Pieced Watercolor Magic
    • Deanna Spingola
A New Slant on Bargello Quilts • Marge Edie
No Big Deal • Deborah L. White
Once upon a Quilt
    • Bonnie Kaster & Virginia Athey
Patchwork Pantry
    • Suzette Halferty & Carol C. Porter
A Perfect Match (revised)
    • Donna Lynn Thomas
Press for Success • Myrna Giesbrecht
Quick-Sew Celebrations
Quilted for Christmas, Book II
Quilted for Christmas, Book III
Quilted for Christmas, Book IV
Quilted Landscapes • Joan Blalock
Quilted Sea Tapestries • Ginny Eckley
A Quilter's Ark • Margaret Rolfe
Quilting Design Sourcebook • Dorothy Osler
Quilting Makes the Quilt • Lee Cleland
Quilting Up a Storm • Lydia Quigley
Quilts: An American Legacy • Mimi Dietrich
Quilts for Baby • Ursula Reikes
Quilts from Nature • Joan Colvin
QuiltSkills • The Quilters' Guild
Quilts Say It Best • Eileen Westfall
Rotary Riot • Judy Hopkins & Nancy J. Martin
Rotary Roundup
    • Judy Hopkins & Nancy J. Martin
Round Robin Quilts
    • Pat Magaret & Donna Slusser
ScrapMania • Sally Schneider
Sensational Settings • Joan Hanson
Sew a Work of Art Inside and Out
    • Charlotte Bird
Shortcuts: A Concise Guide to Rotary Cutting
    • Donna Lynn Thomas
Show Me How to Paper-Piece • Carol Doak
Simply Scrappy Quilts • Nancy J. Martin
Small Talk • Donna Lynn Thomas
Soft Furnishings for Your Home
    • Sharyn Skrabanich

Square Dance • Martha Thompson
Stars in the Garden • Piece O'Cake Designs
Start with Squares • Martha Thompson
Strip-Pieced Watercolor Magic
    • Deanna Spingola
Stripples • Donna Lynn Thomas
Stripples Strikes Again! • Donna Lynn Thomas
Strips That Sizzle • Margaret J. Miller
Sunbonnet Sue All Through the Year
    • Sue Linker
*Surprising Designs from Traditional Quilt
    Blocks* • Carol M. Fure
Threadplay with Libby Lehman • Libby Lehman
The Total Bedroom • Donna Babylon
Traditional Quilts with Painless Borders
    • Sally Schneider & Barbara J. Eikmeier
Tropical Punch • Marilyn Dorwart
True Style • Peggy True
Two-Color Quilts • Nancy J. Martin
The Ultimate Book of Quilt Labels
    • Margo J. Clabo
Variations in Chenille • Nannette Holmberg
Victorian Elegance • Lezette Thomason
Watercolor Impressions
    • Pat Magaret & Donna Slusser
Watercolor Quilts
    • Pat Magaret & Donna Slusser
Weave It! Quilt It! Wear It!
    • Mary Anne Caplinger
Welcome to the North Pole
    • Piece O' Cake Designs
Whimsies & Whynots • Mary Lou Weidman
WOW! Wool-on-Wool Folk Art Quilts
    • Janet Carija Brandt
Your First Quilt Book (or it should be!)
    • Carol Doak

FIBER STUDIO PRESS TITLES:

*The Art of Handmade Paper and
    Collage* • Cheryl Stevenson
Complex Cloth • Jane Dunnewold
Dyes & Paints • Elin Noble
*Erika Carter: Personal Imagery in
    Art Quilts* • Erika Carter
*Fine Art Quilts: Work by Artists of the
    Contemporary QuiltArt Association*
Inspiration Odyssey • Diana Swim Wessel
The Nature of Design • Joan Colvin
Thread Magic • Ellen Anne Eddy
*Velda Newman: A Painter's Approach
    to Quilt Design* • Velda Newman with
    Christine Barnes

PASTIME TITLES:

Christmas Ribbonry •
    Camela Nitschke
Hand-Stitched Samplers from I Done My Best
    • Saundra White
The Home Decorator's Stamping Book
    • Linda Barker
A Passion for Ribbonry • Camela Nitschke

Many titles are available at your local quilt shop. For more information, write for a free color catalog to Martingale & Company, PO Box 118, Bothell, WA 98041-0118 USA.

☎ U.S. and Canada, call **1-800-426-3126** for the name and location of the quilt shop nearest you.
Int'l: 1-425-483-3313   Fax: 1-425-486-7596
E-mail: info@patchwork.com
Web: www.patchwork.com   7.98